The art of life

AF624789

Brittney Sahlin

BookLeaf Publishing

Presentation by *BookLeaf Publishing*

Web: www.bookleafpub.com

E-mail: info@bookleafpub.com

ISBN: 9789357441889

First edition 2023

DEDICATION

To Clara, Hayden, Moose, Liam, Burger King gang and Adde (also always to Ship and Skilla)

PREFACE

The lonely life of a girl

The girl with the books

The words have always been there for me
I used to read like it could save me
Like by pretending I could be somewhere else
When my parents missed me I would be in the library and they'd call and a kind librarian would give me the phone
Oh, to be missed, by them or anyone. What I'd do to have anyone miss me these days
This was before the phones became windows to our lives
For some a window where people look in and out, people watch you and you watch people
For me a window where I look out at life as it happens and nobody ever looks at me
As if life is something to happen only to other but not me, never me
Isn't it natural that I sought a window that was more interesting?
And I started writing books
And I did the thing I still do, base it of my life as I wish it would be
In all my books, I am a character that has friends and goes on adventures
I read too much fantasy and thought watching, watching throught the windows that the were or

are could be enough but it's not and if it not
enough then how can I live
I was a very unhappy child, without an actual
reason
I just always had high expectations and were too
used to watch life throught a window.
To imagine the stories and never experience
them in our world
Very few people live up to the fairytale
expectations my books gave me
And the ones who do are always too far away
and too busy
So I live my life in denial
And tell everyone I'm fine
And live in the fantasy I've made of words that
are all mine

Life's price

Everything has a price, even life
Whatever I’ve done I know I’ve paid for it
Paid for it by having my heart choose this hard
path of life and yet not be satisfied
I’m in the throes of passion, my hands are tied
Everything but my soul has died
I don’t know if I believe in souls, but I hope they
exist
Solely because then I’d have a soulmate to find
And something to look forward to that’s not the
things I left behind
I wish I’d want to flash forward instead of
rewind
But I’m still just here, small, scared and trapped
in my mind
I’m a human but never the right kind
If we’re all deserts, I’m off-brand
My will and motivation are running out like
sands
Like sand out of life’s hourglass hands
Is it weird I want to believe in something bigger
More powerful and immortal than my fragile
human façade
Soon enough this will just be a small part of my
life’s brocade

And all scars will fade
Time won't heal all wounds
But I'd rather have the faded reminders of a life mine lived then the open gaping wounds of a life never lived
And souls might not exist, but people have lived in belief in more dangerous wishes
I know how that sounds
But I do think I can live my life mine on those grounds
And what more could matter?
Than living my life as mine
I will never belong to another person, I better start keep myself as mine
Maybe then I'll be fine
I know I shouldn't whine
But I part of me know I'll rarely be barely fine
But when I am life can be divine
My life is lived in my minds divide
Between pathetic loser and god
Maybe I'm just misunderstood
Maybe I'm not as unique as I've been told
Even if that's how they made me sold
Sold on this idea that there's something there
Something there in me that deserves to be free
Because lately it seems everyone want to be unique, and it makes us all conformed
But I'm different, I argue, as we all do

All these island in the archipelago of compliant independence

Me, the leftover girl

I am a left over girl
Always chosen last
Always in the fringes, on the edges
Allowed to watch and participate but never
being a part of it all
Living on the edges of other people, of things of
groups is hard
Sometimes I wonder what makes it all worth it
But once in a while, something makes me feel
like I could once be a part of something
Something wonderful
Friendship, sports, art
I never found my people
I moved countries to find my people
Because I thought artists and theatre people were
my people but so far university has been like
everything else
Absolutely wonderful, for everyone except me
It's not about the truth, it's about what they don't
se
I came to become who I want to be
But now there's no path to me
No way for me
To be more than a left over girl
Or to be a leftover girl that is appreciated

Always on the fringes and edges
Is it really so surprising I want to be in the centre?
To be seen in whatever way anybody could
So se me in whatever way you would
But would you please se me?
Would you please hear me?
See, hear the leftover girl
The invisible girl
See if I can't surprise you
But if not, am I not a human?
Am I not worthy of being seen or heard?
Because I consider everyone to be
But the people just won't see
We're all human
Just see the lonely, hurt people
Wouldn't the world be more kinder if we look in people's eyes and said, I see you, I hear you
Why does no one want a kinder world for me
Because I see them do it to other people
And the only thing that's different is that I'm me and they are them
The difference is that I'm the leftover girl
And the people know what it's like to be left but to be left you have to have been kept before
No one have ever kept me
I have always kept myself to people and things
Because that's how it works for the leftover girl

Who keeps getting hurt in what’s supposed to a kind world

Unsafe wishes

I hate watching movies that are realistic
Because if the movie is unrealistic
Its so removed from my life I can dream about it safely
It's safe because I know it couldn't be my life
I'm not going to be a popstar, or discover I'm a long lost princess and no matter how much I want it to be true there is no magic on our world
The point is, I know it couldn't be me
But when the movie's about friendship or love or other inspirational bullshit then it hits harder
Because I can't see a reason why I'm undeserving of such things
I am kind, and funny and I accept people and I don't want a lot
But on the other hand I can't see a reason why I'm deserving of anything
I don't think anyone inherently deserves anything in life
But I think we are all given things
Life mostly, never because we want to live but because somehow we came to live
And I do think we all experience it a lot more similar than some people think
We just have different baselines

But why do I feel so shit?
Why can't I appreciate my life?
Why am I not satisfied?
The things I want are not a lot
I just want some goddamm friends
I want people to see me
I want people to know me and to know people
I want people to be the kind of nice you only can be to people you're close to but mostly I want to be that kind of kind to other people
I crave to be able to help people, to know people
I want to have a good soul
I want to be enough, for me but mostly for the people around me who deserve so much more than I can give
I have so much to give, and I just want to be able to give
I want to lower my inhibitions and give freely
But I'm afraid to be left alone with a ripped out heart and soul in my hands

Moving back!

I am moving back and backwards to my
university town
Heavy is not my bag but the realization of how
little I have back home
In the antagonization of my university life I've
forgotten the absence of value my life have here
I must have romanticised it, glorified what I
realistically should have known wasn't here
Friends, a purpose anything that justifies me
getting up in the morning
But all I do is mourning
What I should have had here
But all I have is this fear
What if it's too late, to little? What of it's all my
fault? What if it's just out of my grasp, what if
reaching for it makes me seem presumptuous?
Like I think I deserve it
I still don't know if I deserve it
Can't anybody tell me?
Tell me what I need to hear
That it's all for a good reason
That somewhere, sometime it will be my season
But now I'm still stuck here at this home that
never were my home

This house I know inside out yet never could call mine
I am here and I'm just biding my time
Waiting for a call
Anything at all
I am waiting for someone to remember I exist
Sating at my phone, waiting for any text
I'm a toy in a drawer, that faded magazine at the dentist, those guys in your inbox
Here in case anybody need to be entertained but never good enough to do more than keep around
But is that better than being invisible at what used to be your reason
University is now my old dream
It used to be why I stayed alive
But now I don't really see my way
To live in a world that's not grey
And as the dream begins to fray
I begin to fade
Five days till I'm invisible again
I have nothing, no home nowhere and it should be freeing but how can it be when there's nothing to free me from
It's very clear, being back here
I never really had things like other people
I cling to the things I do have which is why I could never get rid of stuff and why I'll still say people I haven't talked to in years are my friends

I don't know where whatever I have starts or ends
So if I'm to attached or detached
It's cuz I never had anything to be mine
So I never learned how to let go
So I sit here with the hurt from small me I never let go
Like I collected my things in this room
And it hurts me like my overflowing things cluttered my room
My mind is as messed and ugly as my room where when I lived here
But inside me there's a little girl holding it saying this is mine, I don't have much and even if it's ugly and impractical it is and it is mine and it is me and I am it
My room in university has less things but all these things are mine and they are me and I am them, I am still the little girl in my mind but in a less cluttered room but I'm afraid because if I let it go I will lose it all so I cling to any notion of stability, control or me that I can find, cling to anyone who acts friendly and I say too much and too little at the same time and university continue to be as bad as ever but I cling to this last notion of my dream, cling to any sign it's going to get better because I'm clinging onto my life, my reason to not die and if I lose anything I'll lose it all

I’m on the couch, waiting for a call, any call
Please life, give me anything here, anything at all
Because I have nothing here so why did I return

Life!

Life is an interesting thing
No one can ask for, or request to be born, to get the gift or burden of life
Yet we all are expected to be grateful and work for it
I'm 22, why do I still feel like I'm taking care of my parents' child?
How do I exchange my life for one I don't want to leave behind
How do anyone?
Or are all the happy, truly happy people pretending?
Is there no real goal or aim?
Call me nihilistic but that's what I want to believe
Life is a gift, and we are the recipients
So, it's up to us to decide what to do
That's what I want to do.
Se the beautiful things
Find the good things
Experience everything
Do what I want to do instead of following the road paved in front of me
It's not easy
Nothing worth doing really is

But this life, this beautiful and bothersome gift is mine
And maybe I should act more like it
Maybe then I'll find the answers, grow up and be happy for once
Or I'll still feel this way but just like another person, like me
You give me a wase, I can put whatever flowers in it. You give me life and I can't do whatever I want
Because humans live in a web, our actions affect other people and it's a really intricate thing
I've never been part of that in a good way
I'm always hurt or hurting someone else.
But other humans are able to live in this intricate web of socialisation where they constantly affect each other and by god does it look lovely
How I wish I could be a part of that
But I can't
My part will forever be to observe
Maybe that is the plight of the writer
Maybe I just have mythomania
Maybe it's the effects of suburbia
Observing is safer, less harming
If I just watch, I don't need to be charming
But I wish I could be a careless human enjoying the gift of life
I wish I could be the one the stories are about, not the one writing them

I wish I could have a life worth retelling
But no one would remember the gift of my life
except the people who gave it to me and
expected me to be grateful and make something
out of it
And I am doing the best I can but the world is
big and I'm scared and it's all fucking hard and I
didn't sign up for this. I'm sorry for not being a
better person mom and dad, I do appreciate you
and all you've done for me. I'm sorry I can't say
it out loud but I'm afraid I lost my voice because
it's all too big and too important and it would
come out wrong. I'm sorry

Pain is the price

I am in my childhood bedroom
It doesn't feel like home but then again it never did
But now it's not my clothes in the wardrobe, not my things on the shelf or my papers on the desk
It's cleaner, and the window is open more
My parents graciously let me sleep in it until they need it for some thing or other
Just like people will graciously let me be in their life but never be important
There's always something more important
My secret fear is that other people are so much more important to me then I am to them
I know I can't demand things like that but in this aspect my life is so unfair
What do I have to do to be important to the people I care about
How, how can I get them to see some kind of value in me?
Life is not easy but why oh why do mine have to be this hard in this way
I could to whatever if I just could see a way
If all these struggles have a why
But maybe there is no one fits all way or why
Maybe we all are humans trying to get by

And it's not up to the universe or anyone to tell us why
The first step might just be to answer the questions yourself
And trust that if the world or people want to tell you something they will
The road to yourself starts with that first step, then it's one step and then another till you're there
'til you're yourself
But it all starts with a small step
But the smallest step can be the most daunting
And the things we lose is still haunting
The mistakes more so
But what's a human to do
We're built to go, go
Go until we've found it
Whatever your it is
But we put such a value on the things we have to lose
What cost does it have when your heart choose

That is the cruelty of life, fate, the universe. We must put value on things we are bound to lose
But life is about valuing things
Because if nothing means anything how can anything mean anything?

If nothing is worth it how can life, the biggest nothing be worth anything and if it's worth nothing why do we have to pay for it
And pay we do, we pay in the pain, the tears, the blood we shed
That is the price to pay to get to value life
Nothing is worth more than you pay for it. The things what are worth it in life is pained for and the only thing worse than paying for life is numbness
The numbness that comes when you can't pay life anymore
When you can't pain life anymore
When you don't get your worth in life numbness
That fucking numbness
Yeah, I'd take almost any pain to escape it
And there's a small comfort knowing it's all worth it, isn't it?
And maybe it's just what I have to believe to get by
but believing in it all makes me try
Try to be who I am
Try to be in this world I don't understand
With a mind that won't mend
And a will that won't bend
And I'm just waiting for it to break again
What oh what will be left to pick up the pieces?

Happy(ish) new year

Today is new years and I'm afraid
Afraid I'll be as lonely the entire year as I am this day.
Being forced to view people's happiness and to come to terms with how that never could be me
And how I desire it could be me.
People share their year on social media
I see happiness, I see friends, like real friends, not people who can only stand to be around you in big groups at parties.
I see people celebrating and I'm at my parents' balcony watching the fireworks
The same balcony I've looked at fireworks since I was old enough
The balcony I started to escape as soon as I could
Grasped any straw to escape a loving home because I'm weird like that
Does my parents regret it?
Birthing children only to watch them fly away
Because birds have to flee the nest to fly
But does it hurt?
To give everything to someone only to have them run away as soon as possible

I think it would, but then again the only child I'll have is my cat
Happy new year.
People who barely know me wishes it in the phone window and I reply
I'm surprised they haven't forgotten me, honestly
Everyone making resolutions but I can't trust something like that to save me
I wish I could make resolutions and believe I could make them true but it's not in my cards
It's not in my cards and why did I get this deck?
Who shuffled life's cards and gave me the shitty ones.
Everyone says just put your mind to it
They don't get that I don't think I deserve positive changes which makes it kinda hard to work for them. So I'm walking in a haze trying to do what people tell me I deserve.
The boy I loved told me I could be an actress, on the rough seats of the train back home and I decided I would.
I've been told I'm pretty and smart but that's not who I wanted to be, so I chopped of my hair and stopped the academic studying and now I'm nothing
Maybe that's why I'm invisible?
Because no one have told me I could be what I wanted to be.

Except the one time the boy I loved told me I could be an actress
So I moved countries, gave everything up and it's still not enough
When will it ever be?
Next new year?
Or the one after that?
Will any resolution make me make my life one that's enough?
Do I deserve that?
Maybe my new years resolution could be to say I do deserve it?
Yes.
I deserve it and I will work towards it, that's my new year's resolution.
Happy new year

Theatre guy

Theatre guy was the first name my friends had
for the first guy I really loved
They would tease me about him
And I would feel seen
Because I had friends who teased me about
guys, like in the movies
Obviously in the movies, the girl gets the guy
I never really belived he could love me back
then
And then my friends left
He showed up at rehearsal and I was in love
And I became brave and stupid and got burned
And he still get's the same coffee every time and
I still find it encharming
He still pities me just enough to rip up my
eternal cut, the knife being my love for him, the
twist being that he can't even make the rejection
a good thing because he is a good person
Sometimes I feel like he doesn't like me at all
But every time I see him I fall
Can I feel anything that's not laced with hurt
Would it kill him to message me first
And every snap he sends forces a dart
To my better knowing heart

Theatre guy, could we get a new start?
I promise if you tell me about your day
I won't take it the wrong way
Just because I'm dying to hear the three words
you'll never say
Never say to me
Doesn't mean you have to stay away
Even before this all went awry
I know mine was every onesided lovestory's fate
Don't know if you'll ever think of me in a way
other than hate
Because I dared to love someone so great

Not my place/What I would tell you if it was my place

I find the way you get the same coffee every time encharming
You're humble about how perfect you are and as sad as I am about you not seeing your greatness
I find it endearing
I used to hope and yearn
Now I just hope this bridge is not burned
I wish I could kill the part of me that still yearns
Sometimes the heart never learns
Sometimes I wish I could wish you hell
I love how much you love your animals
I kinda died because you were so adorable with your cat the first time I saw you with him
I love your freaking fluffy hair
You're the reason I went to acting school
You're the main reason I stayed in the theatre group for so long
You were the first person I told when I got into acting school
I used to leave my bike at the theatre just to get those extra minutes with you
I brought the supernatural mini book that you gave me on my backpacking trip as an amulet just because you gave it to me

I love you
I hate that I know all the cute stuff you do on
Your youTube chanel
I wish we were cleaner ends
I wish we were better friends
My friends have a shipping club for us
I hate that I still get butterflies whenever your
name pops up
I hate that I love you

Green eyed girl

I am a green eyed girl
I want what I don't have
A life
Love, a love that is returned
Friends
To be taller
To be seen, and heard and appreciated
To make a difference, to matter
I don’t have this and I want it and seeing other people have it makes me jealous, green eyed
My sister is blue eyed
And she has these things
She has always been able to work for things and get them
I wish my work would get me anything
They say jealousy is unbecoming
But my green eyes are simply stunning
But all my life I’ve been running
Running from who I am, running from what has been given to me
Which is brains and beauty
I never cared for either, probably because I never worked for them
So I started running towards who I am but still from what I was given

I tried to work, I really was driven
But nobody saw my work, who I am
My art, caring for animals, being a good fucking person who is worthy
That's what I want people to see
Not just what my parents gave me
And see my sister moose, she could choose who she wanted to be
And I want to be happy
Happy for her and happy for me
But it's hard when she's all these things I want to be
I wonder if she ever wanted to be me

Back to my roots

When I was a child, I was blonde
Then it turned darker like my life
Then I turned it darker like I did my life
I've had almost every colour on my hair
Probably to show that I don't care
Well at least not anymore
When I was young I was particular about my hair
Which is weird because I sucked at taking care of it
But then I parted with it spontaneously in London
The same way I left everything behind to go to university
But now I'm going back to my roots
My hair is blonde again
I do care about it
And I do deserve hair that I like
Even if I liked the wild child, purple haired me
That's not who I am going to be

University, my time to not exist

University was for a long time my second chance
It made me give life another glance
But me or them was on the fence
And I'm the only one who didn't advance
I left everything behind
Just for my life to rewind
Rewind back to the quiet girl I were
Same girl different people not sparing her a thought
What unresolved pain have my childhood brought
God this is harder than I ever thought
Why is my life a war to be fought
And the worst thing is I don't know what's wrong with me
It's like I'm on a different channel than everyone else
Like I'm watching life through a window
Like I'm a ghost, existing yet not, never allowed to have much of an impact but still seeing everything that's going on
I feel like my voice is lost in life's radio static
While everyone else is sharing the studio

When will it me my time to shine
Shine or exist?
Why do I always resist?
Resist, in a way to avoid speaking
Speaking into the void which is what people view me as
If it's not now when will it be my time
My time to exist?

Live, bravely

I have always seen life through a window
Through a window, through books and movies, stories
Maybe that gave me too high expectations
Maybe I don't deserve more then I get
But I want to live in the real world, I can't live behind glass
But if I break the glass
I will have to walk on the shards
I will have to run to catch up with everyone else on the shards of my own window I had to break
Will anyone wait for me to catch up
I wish someone would se my hurt, my feet, my soul, and get why I have to walk slowly and weirdly
But I put up the glass for a reason
To protect me
And I still need that security
Because I have nothing else then my window
I left it all behind
If I don't talk I can't say the wrong thing
If I don't try, I can't fail
If I don't care I can't get hurt
If I don't break my window I won't have to walk on shards

If I don't extend a hand I can't see it being ignored
If I don't put myself out there I don't have to fear
But the thing is I want to feel
I want to live, to exist, to fail and maybe do the right thing some time
Because a life behind a window is not a life and if it's not a life it's not worth it
So I will break my window, I will live, live with all the pain and fear and failure that comes with it because that is the only way you can live, bravely

My nothing ending

No matter how much I pretend
I know how my story will end
It will not be a happy ending
It will not be sad either
Because I know the emotional impact on my
story's end will be the same as my impact on the
world
Nothing
My story will end in a empty nothing
What makes it worth it
I'm just a story like everyone around me
If you ask everyone, their lifes story could
become a book
But what we don't realise is that we wouldn't
read a lot of those books
Important, profund moments in someone elses
life would be boring and mundane to us
Because we are presented to a excessive buffet
of stories made to be better than reality
So, reality, both our and others become boring in
comparison
Boring and trapping, causing us to escape
through fiction
If we make the effort we can be invested in other
people and create stories together

If you look back at it, life, really living life, is
the moments you share with other
But in order to do that you need a mutual
understanding, the kind that comes with being in
reality together and seeing each other stories
instead of fiction
I am a story untold
A lot of people are, I imagine
What are the stories you haven't told?
I wish I could be more bold
I wish I'd know more people's stories
But everyone seems to know each other and I
get stuck in watching reality like a movie
But reality is a movie where I don't really know
the characters, like a movie that's put on in silent
at the dentist
My reality is a movie that's in another language
and everyone else understands it but me
Is it really that weird that I prefer stories that I
can understand?
Where I know the characters and also could
never participate in?
Because that's the worst thing about reality, that
I could be a part of it all but an invisible barrier
inhibits me
Some say it's just in my mind
But those barriers are the worst kind
So I will forego my own story to escape into the
fictional ones

It won’t be sad because I’m an invisible girl
without impact
But on the hopeful side
That my story is completely mine means that I
can write it however I want
If nobody cares, nobody cares
But I can care
I have to care
So, I’ll care about my story
I will write it because I’m the only one who can
If nobody cares
I might as well be the way I want to be
Because I can’t make anybody sad no matter
which way I am
I might as well be the way I wish I could be
I’m going to find and write my story to find the
real me
Because nobody is going to do it for me
What are the stories I’m going to tell?

Imaginary friends

I'm sitting in the kitchen alone
And the saddest thing is that I'm kind of relieved
that no one else is here
Empty chairs at an empty table
It is empty because I don't exist
And neither does the friends I always imagined
myself getting at university
The imaginary friends I left everything for
The imaginary friends I lived for
My university imaginary friends were a greater
comfort when tthere was a hope of them existing
then now that I'm here and sitting at an empty
table, relieved to not have to be lonely in a sea
of people anymore
I am the tree that is invisible in the forest
How could I trust people that are imaginary so
much?
I trusted them to make everything alright but
how could I expect imaginary people to do what
I can't do?
Everyone lied to me about university
They made me picture friends and hard work
and I can't have either
I'm just floating around

Waiting for something, someone to pick me up
from my own ground
But this ground is contractionary deepened by
the expectations I had of the people and things
that won't get me off it
I knnow I'm not owed friends that will lift me
like my imaginary ones would
I need to get over myself and realise that I'm not
the main character in anybody's life but my own
Just because I need lifting doesn't mean that the
people around me have to lift me up
I am responsible of getting myself out of my
own mind
It's only on tv you don't have to work for
anything
I want to work hard but I don't know how
Because I would do anything to turn my
imaginary friends real
I don't even have to let them know how I feel
But I think I need to heal
That is my job and not the people arounds
They rejected me and I wonder on what grounds
My imagination goes negativly out of bounds
I would do anything but I don't know how
No one wants to work hard - but I do
I want to be able to help my
imaginary-turned-real friends
I want to be there for them

I would work long hours if it meant I got to
actually work
Getting to work hard is a privilege I don't have
So I'm going to work as much and as hard as I
can and hope I get paid for it
Because if I want it I have to act like I want it in
order to work towards having it

Fake it 'til you make it

For a long time I didn't dare dream
I didn't ask for a lot of things
And I was happy with what I got
Was my friends the most perfect people?
No but nobody is
I went to school because I should and I did
hobbies because it was fun
It was an easy and sad life
I didn't say I wanted to be an actor because I
didn't think I could ever do it so I couldn't want
it
Because wanting it only makes it sad to not get
it
And it is hard to want something you can't have
I never believed I could have things, so I used to
not want them
And if you don't want things you can't work for
them and if you don't work for them you can't
get them
So I was lost till my theatre guy told me I could
do it and I left everything to become an actor
Now I'm lost at university and in the universe
I'm as lonely as ever and it hurts more because I
do know how lovely it can be to have friends
and I see everyone else have friends

I still don't have things and it hurts because for once I want things and once you start wanting things it hurts more when you don't get it
I don't have what it takes but maybe nobody does
If we all fake it 'til we make it, doesn't that mean that we all made it?
If everyone is faking it, isn't nobody faking it?

Contradictions

I'm a very contradictive person
I think I'm the worst and the best
I love and hate myself
I love life and I want to die yet not
I'm a very pessimistic and optimistic person
I don't want to be loved but I do want to find
love
I want to work and are motivated but just can't
do it
I love reading but the unread books just pile up
I love doing so many things yet do nothing
I love people but never tell them
I never believe I'm worth anything but think I
deserve everything
I'm too quiet and too loud
Say too little yet says the wrong thing
Want so much achieves so little
I'm introverted and extroverted
I never want to be called pretty but sometimes
believe I am
I'm probably wrong
If you think I seem full of myself the only thing
I'm full of is self-doubt

Alive in photographs

My life is actually not sad, at least not in pictures
I have a lot of pictures, moments, with people and at beautiful places
But these are only moments of my very long life
I had a dull, normal childhood in the suburbs
But I was never going to be a settled person
I'm always looking for something else, someone else
I can't do what I'm doing because I'm always craving the next moment I'm allowed to feel actually alive
I'm always chasing and craving the next photograph
Because people and moments leave, they end and in the end they're all fleeting
But I'm too sentimental, yet somehow never enough
I keep all the photograph as a memory of me being alive
Everyone leaves, everything ends. That's the way things go
Everyone else find new people and things but I'm left with a photograph if I'm lucky, just a hole in my heart if I'm not
I'm rarely lucky
I'm rarely lucky but I do have a wall of photographs, moments
The moments that are just moments to other but are what makes me alive
I am defining my life in other peoples moments because I can not exist if I'm not existing in someone else's photographs, their moments
I am not photogenic, or maybe I'm just ugly

If I looked better in photographs would I be alive more?
Would I be a part of people's moments, their
photographs, their world?
I am a lonely soul with photographs of everything that's
ended for me. Photographs of everyone that left and
some that has not left me yet.
Sometimes I wonder when they will

Burger king gang

When I first moved away I had friends
The tv friend group kind
We shared a lot and hung out a lot
The world was closed so there wasn't much to do
In my life as a whole it was a mere moment
But it made me see what life could be
Se I've always been alive in moments, never too long
Everything that makes me alive has other priorities
I should be used to being number whatever now to what is my number one
My friends were here and they opened my eyes and now I'll always see
See what my life could be
They had to move away and now we're oceans apart
And I thought I'd find tv friendship again if I tried
Thought I know how but apparently not
Did they set my expectations too high?
Is our corridor the only decent place I'll live in
Because sharing with anyone else is not the same

I thought it would be but tv lied

Doom scrolling

I wonder how many people see good news in
their carefully manipulative algorithms
How many see bad news?
We live in a depressing world and our social
media makes sure we know how bad it is
My best friend said it was a privilege to read
about bad things and not experience it
I agree
However I do think it's better to try to affect the
world in a positive way than being manipulated
apathetic by the algorithm
Speaking for what's right is more important than
doom scrolling
If I could die for a good cause I would
I think it's a privilege to be in a position to
change anything in the world
We all are screaming into our shared phone void
and the people who are heard are all screaming
about how horrible everything is
I would die to save these people and our world
But I can't
It wouldn't do anything
I'm not privileged enough to make a difference
even if I'd give my life
If I care I care too much

If I'm going to be able to live I have to focus on what I can do, not every single terrible thing in the world
Because I can't live if I feel bad for every single bad thing going on in the world
So I wow to find ways to make the world better and do something
I will try to care about these things in a more non apathic way
Because we are all people and we should care about each other and I want to se the victims of these bad things as people and not just sad stories
And I'd help humans, not just look at the sad situation and just think oh that is so bad
So if anybody reads this try to find a small way to support the causes you believe in and try to be a good human, it will help the world more than doom scrolling

www.ingramcontent.com/pod-product-compliance
Lightning Source LLC
Chambersburg PA
CBHW051738130826
49812CB00033B/909